Frances Tenenbaum, Series Editor

HOUGHTON MIFFLIN COMPANY
Boston • New York 1997

Window Boxes

Tovah Martin

HOW TO PLANT AND MAINTAIN BEAUTIFUL COMPACT FLOWERBEDS

For information about permission to reproduce selections from this book, write to Permissions, Houghton Mifflin Company, 215 Park Avenue South, New York, New York 10003.

For information about this and other Houghton Mifflin trade and reference books and multimedia products, visit The Bookstore at Houghton Mifflin on the World Wide Web at http://www.hmco.com/trade/.

Taylor's Guide is a registered trademark of Houghton Mifflin Company.

CIP data is available.
ISBN 0-395-81371-9

Printed in the United States of America.

RMT 10 9 8 7 6 5 4 3 2 1

Book design by Deborah Fillion
Cover photograph © by Andrew Lawson

Contents

W here would the world be without window boxes? What would become of Main Street if one summer it was suddenly stripped of all the cheerful window boxes that welcome visitors to the heart of town? The postman would have a dull route indeed were it not for the window boxes that brighten his daily rounds; the paperboy would have no target to aim for when he flings the daily newspaper. Apartment dwellers would be totally starved for blossoms without window boxes. No matter where you live, no matter what sort of

The architects equipped this stucco house with window boxes, allowing some needed colorful adornment.

The traditional planting of red geranium, white alyssum, and blue lobelia with a bit of ivy may not be daring, but it is reliably pretty.

quarters you call home, window boxes declare to the world that you've made a substantial effort to please passersby. A flower-filled box is like a welcoming smile. Quite naturally, you want to put your best face forward.

Why, then, are window boxes so often limited to the same old fillers, such as red geraniums, white alyssum, blue lobelia, with a few cascading strands of ivy? It's a pleasing arrangement, but there are so many other possibilities. It's unfortunate — and unnecessary — that there's so little variation in the standard window-box formula, because many other plants will survive, thrive, and look spectacular in this environment. It's time for some Brave New Boxes. Window boxes need to be liberated, and that's what this book is all about.

I also hope to encourage the use of window boxes throughout the land. This is a type of gardening that nearly everyone can enjoy. There is almost no place in the United States where a window box of some sort will not thrive. Even if you cannot claim a square foot of garden space, you can nurture a window

Although the combination of red, white, and blue is perhaps overused in this country, novel plants such as 'Honeysuckle' fuchsia, white chrysanthemums, and blue scaevola provide a fresh view.

This brave box can carry off a riotous combination of varicolored dahlias, zinnias, pansies, and carnations because they are woven together with alyssum, purple petunias, ivy geraniums, and dusty miller.

Daring in both color and content, this dazzling window box is dominated by geraniums, dahlias, impatiens, marigolds, and coleus.

box. Even — or especially — if you are surrounded by concrete you can still enjoy the pleasures of a garden by placing a window box on your balcony, fire escape, or windowsill. Back in Victorian times, these flower-filled boxes were placed inside the window rather than on the outer sill. They were meant to bring the garden indoors.

Wherever you place them, whatever you grow within their confines, think of the delights that window boxes provide; in just a few square feet you can bring

Petunias of the 'Arctic' series boast the longest blooming period, which makes them perfect for window boxes.

a garden into bloom. And window boxes are the perfect project for a beginning gardener, a bite-sized area to distill your design ideas. Everyone should try planting a window box to experience the pleasure of selecting appropriate plants and the joy of watching the little soloists slowly fill in and begin to perform as a chorus. Everyone should learn the skills of nurturing a window box. And, most especially, everyone should experience the pride of collecting compliments from passersby.

Chapter 1:

Choosing the Location

The window-box experience often begins on a spring day with the impulse purchase of the box itself. You plunk down your money, bring the box home, and only then consider where it will dwell and what sorts of plants it will contain. A more sensible approach is to first choose a suitable location for a window box, then select a container that will be appropriate for that position. When those crucial issues have been successfully resolved, you can select plants on the basis of the light available in the chosen location.

Several factors come into play when selecting location. Prominence is very important. Most window boxes are placed on window ledges, for good reasons. First, you can enjoy the flowers from inside the house as well as from the street; a fringe of flowers definitely complements a window sash. And you can't help but notice a colorful container set strategically near eye level. Furthermore, cascading plants such as nasturtiums and ivy geraniums look ravishing as their foliage

Punctuated by lobelia, alyssum, and petunias, these window boxes ensure that color accompanies your ascent upstairs.

Carefully mounted on brackets below a second-story window, boxes can easily adorn a cityscape.

Where direct sunbeams rarely penetrate, ivy and impatiens perform nonetheless.

tumbles luxuriantly from a sill. So ledge-attached window boxes usually host an array of plants that cascade or form low mounds. Taller plants may block the view out as well as the light coming in.

Not all window styles are suitable for window boxes; casements cannot be opened with a window box in place. And if the window doesn't open, watering and pruning will be difficult. If you want flowering plants, you should probably not place boxes on north-facing sills.

If you have chosen a window ledge, you must be able to attach the box securely to the side of the building. If this isn't possible, seek lower ground; the stability of the box should not be taken lightly. Although slapstick comedies and children's cartoons frequently feature flowerpots crashing down on unsuspecting people strolling below, real-life passersby generally fail to see the humor when injured by falling objects, even flowering ones.

Although window boxes were once primarily a window treatment, they've come a long way beyond that association. Nowadays boxes have been successfully adapted to positions both high and low. Quite often a gigantic box brimming with blooms is stationed on the sidewalk in front of a shop, luring potential customers to take a second look. Window boxes hem decks and define patios; they follow stairways up a hill or camouflage the steep grade of a terrace. Filled with begonias or other shade-tolerant flowers, they are positioned prominently on the front porch, flanking the front door. There are few rules governing the placement of window boxes, other than those of good taste, space, and convenience. Window boxes adorn fire escapes, sending trailers showering down or climbers wending upward. Even if you have no space outdoors there's no reason why you can't place a window box inside, as the Victorians did. A box can keep a collection of herbs close at hand on a sunny pantry windowsill. Or it can feature an array of ferns in a front parlor where light levels are low.

Although the conspicuousness of the location is an important consideration in siting your window box, there are other factors to keep in mind. The available light will dictate the plants you choose, as well as the amount of time you have to spend on maintenance. A south-facing window box can nurture that

---

TIPS FOR SUCCESS

Even if your window box is on the shady side of a building, you will get some extra light if there is a concrete sidewalk below or water nearby to reflect the available sunshine. In this situation, with little direct light stress, impatiens and other low-light plants will thrive. But you can try some plants that need more light — just be sure to graduate the heights, putting shorter plants in front and taller ones at the rear of the box.

Light should be the first factor to consider when filling your window boxes, but don't let low light levels stop you; there's always impatiens.

Marching up a series of steps, square boxes lead to a long, lean, flower-filled finale.

favorite trio of geraniums, lobelia, and alyssum as well as sun worshippers with more pizzazz such as gazanias, daisies, evolvulus, and portulaca. However, keep in mind that when window boxes bask in sunny spots, they require watering more than once a day. If you haven't time to attend to their thirst, choose a position that isn't so parched. Also, a box placed in unrelenting sun must be watered carefully to keep the foliage from scorching; water droplets sitting on leaves in brilliant sun can cause burn marks on some plants such as zonal geraniums and evolvulus. During a summer heat wave, sun-drenched window boxes will be wilted by noon if you forget to water, and nothing looks quite as pathetic as a wilted window box.

A low-maintenance box of red geraniums and ivy streamers brightens an otherwise uneventful catwalk.

But usually you are not the only one providing moisture; gentle rains will cut down on your watering time and provide a good, deep soaking drink, encouraging the roots to plunge downward. A raging thunderstorm, on the other hand, can wreak havoc. And remember that it is difficult to keep all but the strongest plants fully foliated and holding their blossoms where boxes are buffeted by wind. Porch roofs and other overhangs will protect your boxes from the ravages of strong sun, heavy rains, and wind. Not only do such locations shelter plants, they also tend to attract people. But when positioning your window box on a porch or under an overhang, just make sure that the box is not directly beneath the roof's drip line. Drips have been the downfall of many a beautiful box.

Chapter 2:

Selecting Containers

The location you select will dictate the size and shape of the container you need. For obvious reasons, window boxes affixed aloft are generally more streamlined than their more down-to-earth counterparts. They are usually wide enough for only a single row of plants, and their length usually matches the width of the window. In the past, ledge-attached boxes were usually made of wood. Granted, wood doesn't last forever, but it will do a fine job for a number of years. If you demand permanence, you can find lightweight versions in all sorts of plastics. Avoid the lizard-green plastic boxes and choose more subtle wood-colored ones that won't clash with foliage or flowers. Metal window boxes tend to rust when the protective coating begins to chip, as it inevitably does.

If your window box is not going to be suspended, it is safe to use a terra cotta or concrete container without worrying about the weight. However, there

If you want to have a display chock-full of flowers, choose a deep box.

On a stucco wall in Mexico City, upright geraniums show off a brilliant blue carved wood box to passersby.

are other issues to address. Terra cotta, concrete, and metal will collect heat in the summer sun and bake tender branches that dangle over the rim of the box. The problem can be solved by selecting heat-tolerant and scorch-resistant cascading plants such as helichrysums, scented geraniums, and verbenas. Or you might site such boxes under a canopy and grow tuberous begonias, impatiens, or other shade-lovers in them.

Wood still remains the material of choice for window boxes. Cedar, redwood, cypress, and teak are all appropriate for the task. Barn boards are currently in vogue due to their rustic charm, although they can't be expected to endure more than a season or two. Even wicker or a long woven basket can function as the shell of a temporary window box if it is lined with plastic; if nothing sturdier is at hand, a heavy-duty plastic bag can be cut to fit. No matter what your box is constructed of, it should have drainage holes so it doesn't become a quagmire in a downpour. A plastic liner should have matching holes.

When they sit on terra firma, window boxes can safely be bulky. They can be wide enough to comfortably entertain two or three rows of plants, and they can be as long as you wish. The height of the box is also open to artistic license, the only rule being that it should balance the other dimensions. Often craftspeople construct window boxes with sides a foot high or more. The plants don't necessarily need all that room for their roots, but the depth looks pleasing and the box tends to dry out less frequently.

TIPS FOR SUCCESS

The greatest chore attendant on having window boxes is definitely watering. To make this duty easier, select deep window boxes that will hold plenty of soil, allowing roots to go deep. If you are having boxes custom built, they can be a foot or more deep, with a wide top tapering to a narrower base. Drainage holes are crucial, especially in areas where summer rainstorms are likely to dump a deluge of water in a short time.

THE RELATIONSHIP BETWEEN THE BOX AND ITS SETTING

Consider the visual chemistry between the box and the setting. You want to display your floral artistry to best advantage and place your mini-masterpiece where it will receive plenty of compliments. Concrete boxes look superb silhouetted against dark buildings, and painted boxes can accent a conservatively colored house just as colorful shutters enhance a whitewashed colonial. Large boxes are usually neutral in hue, but smaller boxes can be any shade under the sun — as long as it doesn't compete with the horticultural performers.

This plain, unpainted box will soon be hidden beneath spilling variegated vinca

Window boxes come in all shapes, sizes, and descriptions. There's no reason why you must cling to the typical rectangular type. Square boxes set on either side of a door might contrast with rectangular boxes under the windows. You can find fancy, carved, sculpted, painted, and otherwise adorned boxes to stretch the limits of your fantasies. But when you consider all those fanciful shapes and designs, keep in mind that the plants are the main feature. A busy box can be a

Beachside bungalows often boast window boxes. Petunias add a collar of color, without blocking the view out.

liability rather than a bonus. Boxes with carved or painted designs on their sides may look seductive in gift catalogs, but the ornament is likely to be completely camouflaged the moment the plants begin to spill over the edge. And overly gaudy boxes tend to compete with the blossoms. Furthermore, brightly painted boxes can dictate the color scheme of the planting if you intend to match hues. Let the plants be the prima donnas.

Purple might seem an uncompromising color. But unlike red, it combines easily with pinks, burgundy, whites, and lavendars.

CHAPTER 3:
SELECTING THE PLANTS

Before you buy plants, consider the location as well as the size and shape of the box. There's no point in planting sun-worshipping geraniums if your window box will be in shade much of the time. And it won't work to cram gigantic cannas into a box that is only four inches wide. As with all aspects of gardening, your creative impulses will have to be slightly curbed by practical constrictions. But there's still plenty of leeway for play.

THE SLIM WINDOW BOX

Ledge-attached boxes and other containers that are displayed off the ground usually require a streamlined planting approach. As a rule, boxes that are four inches wide or less can entertain only a single row of plants that reach modest proportions at maturity. And yet that one row of plants can make a delightfully concise statement.

A study in simplicity, 'Apeldoorn' tulips open in a soldier-straight, carefully syncopated row.

In this restful vista of texture and greenery, boxwood topiaries punctuate a cascade of lacy ivy.

Nemesia, lobelia, and phlox are similar in size and growth habit, so they fall together in perfect unison, making this box very effective.

Although it's fun to seek out rarities, even something as simple as white pansies will look absolutely adorable lined up in a row. In fact, when a narrow box calls for a single row, it is especially effective to choose plants such as violas and Johnny-jump-ups that hold their flowers up proudly above low foliage. In spring, bulbs such as narcissus, tulips, hyacinths, and grape hyacinths also send their blossoms jutting above the leaves.

By the same token, it can be dramatic to emphasize the forms of architecturally striking plants in a sparsely planted row. When you leave some space between plants with fascinating shapes, the silhouettes become particularly conspicuous. The succinct lines of spreading branches and the terse strength of upwardly thrusting stems are emphasized in a single-row window box. Something as common as rose campion *(Lychnis coronaria)* takes on a new splendor when each silver stem can be seen in profile against a dark barn wall.

And there's more to window boxes than pretty flowers. Foliage is worth exploring. A row of umbrella plants *(Cyperus alternifolius),* a ribbon of rosemary, especially the prostrate variety, or a line of myrtle can be truly elegant with plenty of light delineating each plant. Even more dramatic are plants such as boxwood trained into topiary forms.

If a mono-box is not to your taste, try arranging several different kinds of plants. Even a single row of plants need not be limited to one species. Granted, continuity and balance are crucial. In Europe the trend is toward voluptuous window boxes spilling over with a variety of plants. The finished product may appear gloriously unstudied, but in fact a lot of thought has gone into consideration of the various mature heights and flower sizes. Too many odd fellows can look like a hodge-podge. But even the smallest window box can successfully show off a couple of different plants tucked together — as long as the colors are complementary, the growth habits are compatible, and the foliage is comparable in size.

You're on your own when matching flower and/or foliage colors — there are no hard and fast rules. However, you might remember the flower arranger's creed of limiting the number of colors featured in a small space. Color combinations can vary according to your mood and the fashions of the season. If an unusual color scheme appeals to you, there's no reason in the world not to try it. Just keep in mind that some hues deepen when the flowers are grown outdoors. Blossoms selected in a garden center may be whisper pink or light tan in the green-

The shapes of sheared and trained boxwood and ivy complement each other, while yucca provides balance in both color and form.

house, but the moment they enjoy the benefit of unfiltered sunshine, the pinks may brighten to a shocking shade and tans ignite into stark orange. There's nothing wrong with those uncompromising colors, but you need to know what you are going to have before you try to mix and match.

Colors are purely personal, but certain tried-and-true formulas will help in planning the distribution of shapes. In a single-row box, try a configuration of three or four identical upright plants in the center between trailers, acting like bookends, at each edge. Or alternate one or two crouchers, trailers, or low mounds with one or two upstanding plants. To get the best result artistically and to prevent shading out, the difference between heights should not be extreme in a small box.

Although several different players combine in this box, the color palette of the petunias and fuchsias is limited to red, white, and pink, contrasting with purple lobelia.

That is the conventional approach. However, brave boxes of any dimensions can host all manner of shapes and sizes. You might send streamers of ivy or trailing asarina showering several stories down. Or you might go for the weighty look by packing your box with lobelia or pansies that achieve expansive girth. Shock appeal can be delightful, especially in a drab urban setting. If you need to wow the audience, density and vibrant colors will do it.

No matter which avenue you select — the conventional or the startling — you need to know how the plants will behave in the confines of a box. Some folks have beginner's luck, throwing together a random assortment that works as a team. But it's better and less stressful to know the personalities of your players.

Unless it is very deep, a four-inch-wide box best accommodates upright

plants that will not exceed eight inches in height. Keep in mind that the plants you purchase — no matter how tiny they are at first — will grow continually throughout the season. Don't assume that the cute little four-inch plants in cell packs at the garden center will remain that size forever. Always inquire about the mature height of a plant before purchasing it for a window box.

Height is not the only factor for consideration. Width is even more crucial in close quarters; you don't want to invite the horticultural equivalent of Big Bertha to dwell intimately with slimmer bedfellows. And invasive plants should be grown only in their own company. Although it's not always easy to identify a botanical bully, be suspicious of any plant that spreads by underground rhizomes — especially the mints. That sort of takeover personality isn't comfortable for innocent bystanders.

LARGER BOXES

With five or six inches of width at your command, you can usually entertain two rows of plants. Staggering the plants (that is, planting in a zigzag pattern) will keep them from elbowing each other out. In a planter that is twelve inches wide or more, you can stagger three rows.

With so many plants to play with, it's essential to hone your design carefully. The primary rule of thumb is to put shorter plants in front and taller ones to the rear, just as you would in a garden border. If there are three rows, the foremost one often features cascading foliage or forms a low edging. The middle row crouches, and the rear forms a tall backdrop. Again the garden border provides the template — a gradual increase in height is a simple formula that works throughout horticultural design. Staggering allows light to infiltrate to the lower leaves in all the rows.

In a large window box, you can select plants of broad dimensions. Husky plants are fine, and the scaled-up look is necessary to offset the size of the container — small plants such as wax begonias and miniature roses would be lost in a big frame. Plants that achieve two feet in height are ideal for a large window box. But you must provide additional space between them to allow for eventual expansion up, down, and around. Big is beautiful if everything is scaled to the proper proportions.

As long as they are given shade, tuberous begonias will continue to blossom until the end of summer. The compact 'Nonstop' hybrids are particularly appropriate.

THE PERSONALITY OF THE PLANTS YOU SELECT

I discussed specific attributes that dovetail with different-sized boxes. But there are some general traits to look for when you interview plants for their window-box potential.

In the gallery section of this book, you will find all sorts of suggestions for plants that have the right temperament to endure the rigors of life in a container outdoors. But beyond being hale and hardy, window-box plants must also be good neighbors. They can't muscle their brethren for space, they can't tower over them. Only plants that are respectful of one another's turf can happily cohabit in close quarters. And even if you carefully select the most amiable of roommates, the plants must be given sufficient space.

Most people purchase twice as many plants as they can possibly wedge into the space they have at their disposal, but cramming only leads to problems. Granted, you want the display to be gapless, but the end result shouldn't look like a jungle. Don't plant a window box so full that you'll have to thin the plants in a few brief weeks. Air circulation is crucial to prevent disease in such close confinement. Think out your planting plan carefully, just as you would for a garden.

Needless to say, all the inhabitants of a window box must have similar light and water requirements. Plants that require bright sun to bloom will not make a good match with plants that wilt when sunbeams are plentiful. Thirsty plants and drought-lovers will be incompatible. And plants with similar wants and needs should match the location that you've chosen for your window box. It sounds so simple. But so often gardeners are swept away by a pretty combination of plants that they fail to consider the long-term consequences. Design is important, but if only half the plants survive, your grand scheme will be totally defeated.

Traditionally, window boxes are filled with annuals, which do a wonderful job of providing instant gratification. They will kick in immediately and remain blooming over a very long time. But annuals are not the only way to go. Such perennials as lavender, salvias, lychnis, astilbes, and many others make excellent window-box fillers. You probably will want to select plants that look beautiful in rather short order. They need not blossom continually, but they should boast some arresting attribute such as silver foliage or ferny leaves. When the flowers emerge, they are an added bonus. And there's really no reason why a window box must remain static for the entire season. Bulbs and seasonal perennials can work as temporary features if you are willing to replant when their blossoms are spent.

Be creative, look for new plants, experiment to your heart's content. But know the personalities of the individuals you're inviting to dwell in front of your window. Ask a few questions before you purchase. Geraniums and lobelias have ruled the day only because gardeners haven't taken a moment to try other, equally effective window-box fillers.

> **TIPS FOR SUCCESS**
>
> Although flowers are traditional, vegetables and fruits can provide a distinctive touch in a window box. Strawberry runners are particularly attractive cascading over the front of a box. Ornamental strawberries are now available with pink flowers, white fruit, or variegated foliage. Chives, brussels sprouts, lettuce, and peppers are pleasing to behold as well as delicious to harvest.

Chapter 4:

Planting Your Window Box

With your window box in hand and its placement in mind, you're ready to prepare the box for planting. Before you put anything in it, check to be sure it has drainage holes. If it doesn't, you'll have to make them. Holes can easily be drilled into wooden boxes, and you can tap a nail through a terra cotta box to make a hole. A box made of weathered barn boards rarely has snug-fitting boards, allowing some seepage from the sides. If it is not possible to achieve drainage by one means or another (which may be the case with concrete), and if weight is not a pressing issue, you'll have to line the bottom of the box with pebbles to prevent the plant roots from rotting during periods of heavy rain. Mix a few handfuls of charcoal (available at pet shops for use in aquariums) with the pebbles to keep the soil sweet.

Most premixed potting soils will work well in a window box. For obvious reasons, in a box that is to be suspended, you don't want a soil that is heavy with

Long after the narcissus in this window box fade, the pansies will continue to perform.

A perfectly formed composition, with lazy streamers of vinca cascading down, alyssum filling the gaps, petunias and geraniums stationed in the middle, and some cordyline for height.

sand. On the other hand, steer away from seed-starting mixtures and African violet soils. Although they are lightweight, they tend to be fine-textured, so they retain water readily and become soupy in a box. Instead, choose a coarse, humusy soil mixture with plenty of peat and loam. Although it's tempting, convenient, and certainly less expensive to fill a window box with soil straight from the backyard, most unamended home soils are laden with clay and will become compacted in a container. And they are likely to sprout a troublesome crop of weed seedlings. If you prefer to prepare your own potting medium, use equal parts of loam, sand, peat, and compost, adding one cup of bone meal and ten tablespoons of ground limestone for every bushel of soil. If you don't want to battle weed seedlings, sterilize your loam in a 180-degree oven for 30 minutes. Put the mixture through a half-inch screen mesh to sift out the stones.

Moisten the soil mix slightly before you begin to fill your window box. The most efficient and certainly the least messy approach is to proceed in layers rather than filling the box with soil and then attempting to open holes in which to drop the plants. If you are using pebbles and charcoal to promote drainage, start with that layer. Then add enough soil to make a base for the plants to sit on. For a small window-ledge box, only a few inches of soil is necessary beneath the plants. But in a larger box the plants need to sit on a layer of soil equal to half the depth of the box. Be sure to tamp this layer down firmly and level it to a uniformly flat surface before positioning the plants on top. Of course, if your plants have been housed in pots of varying sizes, you'll have to compensate for the different rootball dimensions. In that case, create steps for the plants so their stems are all at the same level.

If you are planting single file in a narrow box, the row should go right along the middle of the container. A staggered configuration is standard for wider window boxes. There's no harm in snuggling cascading plants such as ivies, alyssum, and lobelia close to the edge over which they will be tumbling, with no gap between the rootball and the edge of the container. Taller plants should be placed in the rear.

The correct spacing between your plants depends upon the mature size that each plant is expected to attain and the degree of voluptuousness you prefer. Some plants don't mind being crowded; others prefer plenty of room to stretch. However, the character of your plants will vary according to the space they are

When a window box is densely planted on purpose, each plant will find its own space by tumbling down (the browallia and ivy geraniums) or stretching upward (the zonal geraniums).

allotted. Pansies tucked cheek by jowl will prop one another up, forming small mounds rather than dangling down. Given generous elbow room, sprawlers such as browallia and diascia will expand and look husky as well as showering over the rim of the box. The amount of soil underfoot also affects the eventual size of plants. In a shallow, tight-fitting box, most plants will not reach their full proportions. When a window box is deep and has plenty of dirt, plants flex their muscles.

Spacing depends upon the box's dimensions and the repertoire of plants. It's difficult to give hard and fast rules besides cautioning you to leave ample room for plants to fill in. Don't fret if the window box doesn't look lush at first. Even

Wax begonias and coleus peacefully coexist, having been planted in the proper zigzag configuration.

the most generously spaced window box will look ravishingly full within a few weeks after planting. In the meantime, your neighbors will understand. The post-man will sympathize. Every sane and sensible visitor will know that your win-dow box is destined for future glory.

So, with your plants neatly positioned, you are ready to fill in with soil. Scoop your planting mixture in generously all around the roots; then, with a pen-cil, a slender stick, or your finger, tamp the soil down firmly between all the plants and around all the edges. Unfilled or loosely filled spaces are the nemesis of many window boxes, for that allows the roots to dry out, and the results can be fatal. It is crucial to cram the soil firmly into all crevices and crannies. Then pick up the window box and bang down gently but firmly on the potting table a few times to encourage the soil to settle. Add more soil if necessary. The final step is to spread soil evenly on top, leaving half an inch to an inch of space (depending upon the size of the box) between the soil level and the rim of the box for watering. That space is an important factor in the success of your win-dow box. If you fail to leave sufficient space for watering, the box will dry out with perplexing frequency. Then again, if the soil level is too low, the box will serve as a reservoir for water in a downpour.

Most window boxes do not need mulching or top dressing. Although you might see some naked soil when the box is first planted, it will be covered as the plants expand. Some boxes, however, are purposefully sparse. If you've chosen an architectural look and planted with plenty of space to silhouette each stem, there's nothing wrong with leaving the soil unadorned. But you may prefer to top-dress with pebbles, especially if your box hosts alpines or rock-garden plants. For a more dramatic look, use polished stones. Obviously, such weighty fillers are pos-sible only if the box is not going to be suspended. Other mulches can be used, but mulching is not really necessary. And you don't want to make it more difficult to water the plants.

A window box that silhouettes a few slender-stemmed plants could be adorned with a groundcover that hugs the soil. Why not invite a handsome creeper such as pearlwort, ajuga, creeping pennyroyal, mazus, or selaginella to carpet the soil? The greenery will prevent the soil from drying out so frequently and the finished effect is quite handsome. All you need do is tuck a smidgen of one of the above-mentioned groundcovers at each end of the window box. No

This springtime window box features a cheerful though fleeting performance by primroses, narcissus, and tulips.

Three apple red geraniums fill the center of this box, leaving plenty of room for alyssum to expand into a wispy cloud.

need to plant between all the taller plants. The groundcovers that I've mentioned will carpet the window box with amazing speed.

If you can, try to schedule your window-box planting to coincide with a drizzly or cloudy spell. However, if your gardening weekend is radiantly sunny, it is wise to throw a lightweight cloth over the newly planted box when the sun is pounding down. After all, you've shocked the plants a bit in the repotting process; even the seemingly uninvasive transfer to a window box stresses the roots slightly. Rather than asking the plant to deal with sun trauma while its roots are recovering, you should offer them some shelter.

Along with shelter, provide drinks a little more often than you will when the plants are comfortably established. Water the newly planted window box generously immediately after you've finished potting. It's important to make certain that the water soaks all the way down. Then, if the weatherman doesn't promise precipitation, water twice daily. Do it gently. Break the stream of water with a spraying nozzle, or rose. You don't want to wash away all the soil that you have so meticulously wedged into place.

Window boxes that sit on the ground often have small wooden or terra cotta feet so the drainage hole is free to do its job. This isn't essential, but it does help. And a box can look quite handsome on raised supports, if they are stable.

> ### TIPS FOR SUCCESS
>
> Many seasoned window-box gardeners claim that the secret to a lush and lovely display is to snuggle a number of plants close together. When you plant this way, the roots have to grow down rather than out, and the plants grow taller than they do if there is plenty of room between them. Be sure to water generously and fertilize often to compensate for the cramped quarters.

Aside from watering, you can now spend some well-deserved time sitting back and admiring your handiwork. The box may look a little sparse for a time, but if you planted with inspiration and if you spaced the plants with an eye toward the future, good things are bound to happen. In a very short time, your window box is destined for glory.

Chapter 5:

Window-Box Upkeep

You're not totally free to lounge on your chaise and sip lemonade after your window boxes are planted. After all, your boxes hold living, growing things, and your first goal is to make certain they remain that way. Not only must you quench their thirst on a regular basis, but strategic pruning and grooming are necessary to ensure that the display will fetch compliments all season long. A well-attended window box will draw all eyes; a neglected one is a sad sight.

Watering

Watering is the chore that must be done most frequently and regularly. When window boxes are positioned in the sun, they tend to dry out quickly. Compact, shallow window boxes require a drink at least once a day. If you go on vacation for a weekend, you're likely to receive a very wilted welcome when you return

When a window box is suspended aloft, windows that open easily are essential for quenching the plants' thirst.

If you pinch coleus when you plant, it will willingly expand rather than follow its natural tendency to shoot straight upward.

home. The tried-and-true window-box plants will forgive some lapses in water-ing, but you shouldn't try to push their good nature. If possible, ask a neighbor to give them a drink while you're gone. I always leave a full watering pot handy for anyone who might feel inclined to come to the aid of a thirsty window box. Even if a helpful stranger drowns the box in water, it's better than attempting to revive seriously wilted plants.

Watering a window box is certainly not a difficult science, but this critical chore requires a few words of explanation. Your life will be much easier if your window box never becomes bone dry. Once a window box has dried that much, its quite difficult to soak the bottom layer of soil again. So regular watering is the key to success. Once a day will usually do it, although window-ledge boxes may need water twice daily in the heat of the summer, especially when the tem-perature soars and there isn't a cloud in sight. Windy days also intensify the need for water, making twice-daily applications necessary.

As I mentioned earlier, it's imperative that your window box be easily acces-sible for watering purposes. If the box is attached to a sill, you should be able to open the window and water from indoors. However, if your box hangs over a busy city sidewalk, check the street below for pedestrians before doing so. No one appreciates an unannounced morning shower.

When you water, use a rose or attach a water brake to soften the gush from your hose. Most window-box plants don't mind having their foliage sprinkled as you water, but you may risk scorching the leaves. If possible, water in the morn-ing or evening rather than at high noon or when the sun's rays are falling directly on leaves. Even those old standbys the zonal geraniums have been known to scorch when water sits on the leaves in direct sun. And there's an additional bonus to watering in the morning or evening: your efforts will be more productive. The water will seep down all the way rather than filtering only an inch or so below the surface before transpiring. Deep watering encourages the roots to plunge down rather than creeping along at the surface, which leads to frequent wilting.

Of course, a plant-packed window box will dry out more often than a sparsely planted one. And certain plants dry out more quickly than others. Verbenas, chrysanthemums, densely planted petunias, and violas tend to wilt with little provocation. Geraniums, helianthemums, and morning glories rarely wilt unless water is withheld for an uncomfortably long time, such as two days or more.

*Nasturtiums offer a season full of color but require a bit of care. Pruning is essential,
as is removal of yellowed leaves.*

When you water, fill the box to its rim once and then leave well enough
alone. No need for repeated fill-ups. If you've left the recommended inch at the
top of the box, a single visit with the watering pot should do the trick.

Needless to say, you don't have to water if Mother Nature is providing
enough. However, too much water is not good. I've already discussed positioning your window box so it isn't subject to the full brunt of cloudbursts or of roof
runoff after a raging thunderstorm. Those drainage holes are important when a
rainy spell is stalled right over your house for a week or more. Also you should
discourage young children from watering the window boxes at whim. After a tor-
rential downpour or a week of unending precipitation or a five-year-old nephew's
watering binge, check to make sure that the soil hasn't washed out of the boxes.

A densely planted window box will require water more than once a day during the heat of the summer.

If petunia flowers are nipped off soon after they fade, the plants are encouraged to produce more buds.

If daily watering just isn't possible for one reason or another, do not despair. There are alternatives. Drip irrigation is the standard means of watering gardens in parts of the country that receive scant precipitation. There's no reason why this system can't work for a window box — at least for the grounded versions; it just isn't convenient or practical to attach window-ledge boxes to a soaker hose. But sizable boxes sitting safely on terra firma could easily have soakers quenching their thirst.

If you look carefully through garden catalogs, you can find plastic window boxes that have a water reservoir hidden in a false bottom. They may be expensive, but this particular contrivance is well worth the investment if it allows you to put window boxes in places that would otherwise be impossible. Less costly, not quite as effective, but nonetheless very helpful are ceramic, plastic, or glazed terra cotta window boxes fitted with trays underneath that collect the excess water, to be slurped up when the soil is thirsty. You can also purchase wick waterers connected by slender hoses to a plastic reservoir. Any device — mechanical, human, or otherwise — that helps you water a window box is worth investigating.

FEEDING

A newly planted window box will not require feeding for quite a while. After all, you've just given the roots quite a generous quantity of all sorts of good nutrients in the potting soil. Your plants are feasting, and additional fertilizer could cause problems. However, halfway through the summer, when your window box is growing at full speed and the plants have intertwined into a dense jumble, feeding is necessary. Use 20-20-20 or any balanced fertilizer and dilute it according to the directions. From midsummer onward, you might feed once every two to three weeks with excellent results. However, don't assume that if a little fertilizer works, more is better. As far as fertilizer is concerned, your plants can definitely get too much of a good thing.

PRUNING

Although watering is the most pressing issue, another important element of window-box cultivation is pruning. Not all plants are self-branching. With plants that do not have this laudable trait, it is very helpful to pinch out the growing tips in their youth to encourage a full display later on. Many experienced gardeners pinch back all their plants when they put them in a window box. If a plant stands a foot tall, you might cut it back by half to coax branching from the base. Don't think you're impeding progress; it is the root system that governs the plant's growth. And you're not diminishing the roots when you prune the top.

Despite the temporary setback, pruning will lead to a bigger and better dis-

Vigilant grooming is necessary for any window box, especially for nasturtiums and other bloomers that hold on to their spent flowers.

TIPS FOR SUCCESS

Start pinching your plants back
early on to encourage them to
sprout new branches. Many
gardeners pinch back their plants
as they put them in, especially
when setting out pansies, violas,
petunias, and snapdragons.
Pinching also will spark a second
flowering for many bloomers,
and it's amazing how rapidly
plants recover from even the
severest haircut.

play, for every cut will encourage the stems to branch into two
stems. Some plants, like lobelias, just naturally divide without
any intervention whatsoever. Others, such as verbenas, salvias,
and impatiens, need to be disciplined or they'll send a single
spindly stem shooting straight up. Many plants are at their best
for a length of time, but then the show begins to deteriorate.
Pansies look absolutely ravishing for a month or more and then
begin to get leggy. The moment they start to stretch, prune
them back so they can start a second flush of growth. And pansies are not the only ones that require this treatment. Trades-
cantias, verbenas, and petunias all require pruning to continue
looking their best. In general, pruning does no harm and can
lead to some beautiful results.

GROOMING

To create the most splendid scene possible in your window box, you should
remove all dead branches, dig up any plants that have failed to survive, and
remove leaves that have yellowed or browned. If there are gaps large enough for
a substitute plant to fill, slip it in early in the season so it has time to catch up
with the others. Tidy your box on a weekly basis, and give it a critical inspection
every time you water. Check for aphids and apply insecticidal soap the moment
those pesty little varmints appear. Don't wait for the infestation to reach mam-
moth proportions. And rather than relaxing when the first application of insecticidal soap does its job, you should continue to cast a vigilant eye on the leaves.
Aphids never totally disappear after the first shot — persistent warfare is always
necessary.

Some bloomers such as petunias, snapdragons, and salvias should be dead-
headed just after a flower stalk reaches it zenith. It might seem as if you're snipping off the finale of a fantastic show. But in reality you're investing in future
flowers. Another practice that prolongs the blooming binge is removal of the
flowers before they start to set seed. When a plant is working to produce the next
generation, it puts less energy into flowers.

In some cases, you will have to replant your window box. Don't hesitate to start fresh the moment a seasonal window box begins to flag. Spring bulbs are particularly transient. When narcissus flowers wilt, long before the foliage starts to brown, throw them out and replant the box for the next season. Seasonal boxes provide several opportunities to try your hand with different casts of characters. They hone your window-box skills.

WHEN SUMMER IS OVER

All good things come to an end, and summer is no exception. By fall your window box will probably have reached its peak of beauty. Of course, when autumn arrives, it's essential to keep an eye on weather reports in anticipation of chilly nights. You can prolong your autumn display by draping the box with a sheet or pillowcase when frost is predicted. If you haven't protected your plants, or if the weather folks failed to predict a frost (it's been known to happen), the sad remains should be removed posthaste. There's nothing quite as depressing as a frost-smitten window box reminding you of your sins and nature's might.

After a killing frost, your window box should be emptied of soil. If left to freeze and thaw through the winter, that soil can wreak havoc with the container, no matter what it's made of. Once the soil has been removed, you can put in hardy mums or flowering kale, leaving the plants in their original pots but setting them into the window box as if it were a cachepot. Later you can fill the box with greens for the holidays. Pines, fir and holly boughs, together with branches laden with red berries, will look cheerful for several weeks.

Later, when the snow flies, it's time to call it quits and take down your window boxes for the season. Snow may be too much of a burden on the brackets of ledge-affixed boxes. And the box may cause drifts to settle against your windowpanes. No matter how heavy they are, terra cotta and concrete boxes should be brought indoors so that snow and freezing weather don't cause chipping or cracking. Clean your boxes thoroughly, wash them out with diluted chlorine bleach if you want to make absolutely certain that they aren't haunted by any of summer's pests, and store them in the cellar or garage until the next planting season arrives.

Chapter 6:
Ideas for Window Boxes

In the crusade to liberate the world from the plants that have predominated in window boxes for far too long, you might consider creating a theme window box. Your theme could be as simple as spring bulbs or as sharply focused as plants to attract butterflies. Sometimes the location dictates the theme; for example, a window box situated beneath a canopy of trees must be devoted to shade-loving plants if it is to thrive. In most situations, however, you have plenty of leeway to dream up an original theme.

Rather than limiting your possibilities, themes exercise your creativity. If color is the important issue, you could concentrate on plants of a certain hue. Or you could make it your mission to throw every color of the rainbow together. Loosely followed or stringently enforced, a theme will give you a goal and make your window-box odyssey quite entertaining as well as educational.

Miniature roses in a box can echo the larger roses in the garden.

Bees and butterflies will be drawn to this window box filled with verbena and petunias.

SUN- OR SHADE-LOVERS

Most plants recommended as window-box fare, including the ever-popular geranium, lobelia, and alyssum combo, will thrive in any location that receives at least half a day of bright light. The list is long, the possibilities many. Heliotropes, gazanias, snapdragons, dahlias, coleus, cosmos, dianthus, hibiscus, nasturtiums, petunias, poppies, geraniums of all descriptions, marigolds, verbenas, and zinnias are among the legendary sun-loving window-box performers. However, you might be a little daring and try something different. Persian violets, African daisies, ornamental peppers, nemesia, celosia, lantana, scaevola, browallia, helichrysums, and asarinas are all worth exploring in a sunny spot.

As any gardener learns, there are sunny locations and then there are sun-*drenched* spots. If you live beside water, chances are that window boxes on that side of the house will bask in brilliant sun a good part of the day. If your house is on the beach, the sun's rays may be scorching. On the terrace of a city high-rise, unbuffered by other buildings, the sun's radiance can be overwhelming. Gardeners in the Southwest, especially, find that their window boxes receive intense sun most of the time. In those locations you should select plants that are adapted to the climate. Desert plants, Mediterranean plants, aromatic herbs, and alpines will all stand up to unrelenting sun. Most especially, rosemary, helichrysum, lewisia, felicia, convolvulus, evolvulus, nierembergia, myrtle, yuccas, agaves, helianthemums, sedums, pimpernel, and lithodora will all perform well.

We usually think of window boxes as basking in the sun, but there's no reason why a shady location can't play host as well. In fact, gardeners who have window boxes in the shade need not be quite so ever-ready with their watering pots. But you will have to plant with the low light levels in mind, and the repertoire of shade bloomers isn't quite as long as the list of sun-lovers.

Most people turn to impatiens if flowers are their heart's desire for a shady location. But equally suitable for the shade and just as eager to blossom as the standard *Impatiens wallerana* hybrids, available in garden-center cell packs, are the New Guinea hybrid impatiens, which have colorful foliage as well as a rainbow of flower colors. A little more obscure but occasionally available at garden centers are the dwarf impatiens, sometimes known as the Hawaiian series. Double impatiens are beginning to appear in the garden centers; they tend to be com-

In autumn, champagne-colored chrysanthemums tarry long after frost, lengthening the window-box season considerably.

Shaded window boxes need not lack flowers. Both fuchsias and impatiens will thrive.

Although they are fleeting, spring bulbs provide a shot of vibrant color right when you need it most. The display will linger if the window box sits in partial shade.

pact and punctuated by a plethora of blossoms that bear an uncanny resemblance to miniature roses. Impatiens may be the blossoming mainstay for shady window boxes, but you will need to visit them often with your watering pot. They're heavy drinkers, but impatiens will revive from a sensationally deathlike swoon within a few minutes when you quench their thirst at last. In addition, pruning will encourage a full, gapless display.

In spring, flowering bulbs stage quite a satisfactory performance in a shady location. And later in the season violas, pansies, and Johnny-jump-ups in partial shade have a longer blossoming period than they do in full sun. Not only do they flower enthusiastically, but they wilt less frequently; in bright light you can spend an inordinate amount of time fetching water for violas.

Similarly, primroses put on an impressive blossoming display in shade and are far easier to maintain than those grown in sunny locations. Although the *Primula veris* hybrids are generally called into service, all sorts of primroses will perform admirably in shade, although their blossoms usually cease when the weather becomes hot.

Depending upon the degree of shade that you are dealing with, other flowering plants will also do well. Try filling your window box with lady's-mantle, astilbes, tuberous begonias, fuchsias, and ajuga if you crave blossoms. Or, if you are content with colorful foliage, plant caladiums or rhizomatous begonias. Before you dismiss ivies with a yawn, check out all the colorful new hybrids available with spotted, marbled, silver, and gold-flecked leaves. You could definitely plant a window box solely in ivy and not be bored for an instant. Not only that, you wouldn't be busy — ivies require little care.

COLOR THEMES

You can choose any color of the rainbow and devote a window box solely to that hue. In the age of the white marigold and the lavender impatiens, there's scarcely a color that isn't represented at your local garden center. White window boxes are currently in vogue, especially if they mix luminous white blossoms and silver foliage to create a ghostly effect. A particularly impressive combination is white-blooming *Nierembergia* 'Mont Blanc' and *Verbena tenuisecta* 'Alba' combined with the hoary leaves of the dwarf licorice plant, *Plecostachys serpyllifolia*. Further

forays into white themes could utilize white heliotrope, petunias, and dahlias, white-flowering, silver-leaved yarrows (such as *Achillea clavennae*), and the perennial snapdragon *Antirrhinum molle.* For foliage, you might tuck in one of the many silver-splashed ivies, such as 'Glacier'. With an abundance of sunlight, you could easily complement the flowers with the hoary foliage of *Artemisia stellerana* 'Silver Brocade'.

Feel free to choose a color that strikes your fancy and plant a box devoted to exploring that shade. Against a white wall, an all-purple window box stands out, especially if you combine various purple pansies, petunias, heliotrope, verbenas, blue salvia, and lobelia. Combining plants in a limited color range is great fun, but you should maintain an ounce of prudence while your imagination roams. An all-red window box will appear very hot in midsummer, as will a brilliant yellow one. That's no reason not to play with the bright colors, but con-

A trip down any Main Street in America will quickly reveal that red, white, and blue is the most common theme for window boxes.

sider buffering them with plenty of green foliage. Blues, pinks, and lavenders are more restful shades for a sizzling season.

One note of caution. When you select plants for a mono-box, it's best to see the actual flower hues before you buy. Photographs in mail order catalogs may misrepresent the intensity of a yellow or render a true-blue blossom as a much paler, pinker shade. You want to be certain that all the color variations you've chosen combine harmoniously.

Rather than concentrating on one color, most window boxes include a pleasing medley of two or more different shades. Selecting blossoms that work together is definitely an interesting challenge. The patriotic red, white, and blue grouping may be overdone, but it definitely works. Try red verbena, white lantana, and blue salvia for a change. Other successful mixtures are purples played against pinks or yellows with blues or almost any color with white. Brave new

Devoted solely to petunias, this mono-planting certainly doesn't look boring, because the color combination is so vivid.

boxes have been known to combine screaming magenta and pumpkin orange without too many complaints from the town fathers. When you make a strong statement, people will respect your courage and admire the result.

Fragrance

Color may speak loudest to the world at large, but window boxes can provide all sorts of other pleasures. Just think of the attributes you might wish for in a box of flowers sitting just outside your windowsill. Chances are that fragrance is high on your list of desired traits.

A box of fragrant flowers and foliage on the windowsill is a dream come true. And it's so easy to create. When sunbeams fall heavily on heliotrope and fragrant verbenas such as 'Silver Anne', the aroma naturally floats indoors on the breeze. Although fragrant foliage doesn't usually impart its charms unless you rub the leaves, bright sun rays can release the scent of herbs that are well endowed with essential oils, such as rosemary, basil, marjoram, and lemon verbena. In fact, many leaves that emit lemon scents make splendid container plants. These include lemon balm, lemon thyme, lemon-scented geraniums, and lemon grass. Although lemon grass is no raving beauty, it might work in a box if camouflaged by other, more attractive plants.

Be careful when mixing fragrant flowers. Perfume is a tricky business, and too many scents together may clash. Steer away from heavily fragrant flowers such as tuberoses and night-blooming jasmine *(Cestrum nocturnum),* for their aroma can be overwhelming when it comes rushing through an open window. The safest method is to take the perfumer's tactic and employ one "top note" such as jasmine, trachelospermum, hoya, or gardenia and mix it with subtler scents such as roses, scented geraniums, heliotrope, sweet peas, or Persian violet. The resulting redolence will be delightful.

Culinary Boxes

Just think of the convenience of growing a window box filled with savory herbs within easy reach of your pantry. You simply open the screen, snip off some thyme or basil, and sprinkle it into the spaghetti sauce. Thyme is one of the best

window-box herbs, and it comes in so many different flavors. You could plant a medley of caraway thyme, golden lemon thyme, English thyme, Spanish thyme, and celery-scented thyme. Or you could invite a broader selection of frequently employed herbs to live together. Marjoram, oregano, savory, basil, and tarragon are all sufficiently compact to dwell comfortably in a window box. And let's not forget the famed Scarborough Fair combo of parsley, sage, rosemary, and thyme. In fact, several of the fancy-leaved culinary sages are capable of adding a little spice to your window box — try golden, purple, or tricolored sage. The best rosemary for the job is the trailing version, *Rosmarinus officinalis* 'Prostratus'. As a bonus, this rosemary is frequently smothered in sky blue blooms.

Most herbs dwell quite happily in the confines of a box. Mints, however, do not make good bedfellows. They can't be trusted more than a minute in polite company, before they start elbowing out all the other plants. Give them a box of their own, where they can spread in all directions.

ATTRACTING WILDLIFE

Few gardeners want to lure deer to their front door, but you might like to coax butterflies and hummingbirds to come closer. To attract butterflies, try passionflowers, pentas, sedum, ageratum, candytuft, cosmos, marigolds, phlox, mignonette, zinnias, sweet alyssum, or scabiosa.

Hummingbirds are partial to blossoms that are brilliant red and those with long tubular throats. Fuchsias definitely top their list of favorites. They are also attracted to impatiens, nicotiana, penstemon, petunias, phlox, red salvia, nasturtiums, and geraniums. Hummingbirds are not particularly shy and will usually take the lure. Just plant your window-ledge box, get out your binoculars, and enjoy the entertainment.

DROUGHT-TOLERANT PLANTS

Instead of hiring a window-box waterer or installing drip irrigation, you can try another tactic in the battle to keep window-box plants from drying out. You can fill a box with drought-tolerant varieties. True, the typical window box is not filled with cacti and succulents, but they should thrive in that type of growing

Another solution for shade is tuberous begonias. Be sure to place the box in a dry location — begonias detest having damp toes.

space. Of course, it's impossible to predict the weather in most parts of the country, and the summer might be punctuated by heavy rainstorms, resulting in an epidemic of general rot. But during most summers, a window box filled with drought-tolerant plants in sandy soil would do just fine. Put in sempervivums (hens-and-chickens), lewisia, agave, euphorbias, or species pelargoniums. Consider enhancing the overall effect by top-dressing with pebbles. Thus planted, your window box should need watering only twice a week in most cases.

Autumn Window Boxes

Summer is so fleeting — who can be blamed for hoping to extend the window-box season into mid- and late autumn? Chrysanthemums are definitely old standbys for the autumn window box. Granted, they begin to look tired after a while, and their show shouldn't be prolonged past its peak. But they do an excellent job of providing a glorious display for many weeks after the annuals have succumbed to frost.

Flowering kale is a fine filler for late-fall window boxes throughout the colder regions of the country. Kale has a habit of pushing itself out of the soil, but its naked ankles can be rather intriguing if you show them off as a design feature, making the effect seem carefully planned. For a different twist, add Cape heather as an accent. Although heather, kale, and chrysanthemums will carry the show, foliage plants, such as 'Gold Leaf' ivy and euonymus, can also have quiet appeal.

Several herbs remain green until the snow flies. Horehound, winter savory, parsley, culinary sage, and hardy violets stubbornly refuse to call it quits. You can harvest them until the bitter end of the growing season and beyond. Prolong the theme as long as you wish. However, keep in mind that the soil in your window box shouldn't freeze and thaw repeatedly, for that will damage the container.

CHAPTER 7:

A GALLERY OF PLANTS

Window-box plants are an eclectic bunch. If there is one common goal, it is that they should be sufficiently exciting to capture the attention of passersby. And they should continue to turn heads over the longest period of time possible.

Long dominated by a few flowers that have reigned supreme, window boxes need a breath of fresh air. So the following gallery offers some suggestions that aren't standard window-box fare. And I've skipped over some of the plants you've seen again and again — why reiterate the obvious? Instead, give the following plants a chance. Of course, there are many other plants that may work well, and new performers are introduced every year. Be creative.

Petunias come in an incredibly broad range of colors and blossom reliably throughout the summer.

■ **AGAPANTHUS** / Lily-of-the-Nile
Height 2 to 3 feet
Sun or partial shade

With its tall blue flower spikes towering above tidy clumps of grasslike foliage, agapanthus can make a dramatic window-box plant. The foliage forms neat but dense clumps, which may take up too much space, crowding out other plants. So for window-box purposes, agapanthus is often used alone, keeping its own company. If you want an agapanthus that you can combine with other bedfellows, look for the dwarf hybrid 'Peter Pan'. Standing only 1½ feet tall, it also has dramatic blue blossoms, but its compact ways leave plenty of room for neighbors.

Agapanthus can grow in full sun or partial shade. However, they're sensitive to bright sun when first making the transition from indoors to out. To prevent unsightly browning and wilting of the foliage, put your plants in the shade outdoors for a few days before planting them in the window box.

■ **ARCTOTIS** / African Daisy
Height 1 foot
Sun

This member of the daisy clan boasts silver leaves that squat compactly around the base and rarely wilt unless severely water stressed. Throughout the season the foliage is crowned with daisy-shaped flowers on foot-long stems. So far the color range is limited to pinks and oranges. However, be cautious when playing with those colors. 'Wine', the common pink variety, looks quite tame in spring but turns a much brighter shade under summer sun. And 'Flame', the common salmon, deepens to dark tan by midsummer when grown outdoors. You can snuggle either 'Flame' or 'Wine' closely between other window box neighbors. Arctotis will not expand much sideways.

Agapanthus africanus 'Alba' should be grown in a large window box, where its grassy leaves have plenty of room. For smaller spaces, choose the miniature 'Peter Pan'.

- **ARTEMISIA**

Height 10 inches and up, depending upon variety
Sun

Wonderful things happen when you combine silver artemisia with a white-flowering plant like *Nierembergia* 'Mont Blanc' to create a frosty window box. If you are light-handed with the watering pot and scant of space in your box, try *Artemisia schmidtiana* 'Nana'. If you have a little more room to play with, look for the broader-leaved dusty-miller lookalike, *Artemisia stellerana* 'Silver Brocade'. Ferny, lacy silver foliage is the attribute for which artemisias are famed. Flowers are not this plant's forte. In fact, you should snip them off, for they usually detract from rather than further the display.

- **ASTILBE**

Height 5 inches to 2 feet
Shade or partial shade

Although window-box plants ought to bloom throughout the season, we make a few exceptions where shade is concerned. Astilbes perform primarily in July. But even when these lovely plants aren't crowned by pink, white, salmon, or red plumes, the ferny foliage is quite elegant. And astilbes are not solely for shade. They'll do well in sun if you increase the water to their thirsty roots. Choose any color you desire; they're all appropriate. If space is at a premium, select the wee *Astilbe chinensis* 'Pumila'.

- **BEGONIAS**

Height 6 inches to 2 feet, depending on variety
Shade

There are begonias galore, and most types, with the exception of the rexes, which are too finicky, will work just fine in a window box. The semperflorens, or wax begonias, are the most commonly used outdoors. Their foliage isn't particularly exciting, but the rosebud-like flowers are produced in quantity. Semperflorens begonias will withstand some sun. Second in popularity for window boxes are tuberous begonias. These must have shade, but they blossom more dramatically

When astilbes, such as this pink Astilbe × arendsii, *are grown in shade and given ample water, they make fine window-box plants.*

Tuberous begonias display all the panache of roses with a fraction of the fuss.
However, mildew can set in if your window box doesn't have good air circulation.

Browallia speciosa *'Major'* can be encouraged to sweep downward or stand straight up, depending upon its placement in a window box.

than any of their relatives. Among the best of the tuberous types for window boxes are the compact 'Nonstop' series, which are available in a range of white, yellow, pink, red, salmon, and orange. The roselike, many-petaled flowers can reach 3–4 inches in diameter.

If you want stunning foliage, try angel-wing or rhizomatous begonias. Like their tuberous cousins, they prefer shade. With their intriguing leaf markings and elegant leaf shapes, they fill low-light areas beautifully. The flowers aren't as exciting as those of the tuberous begonias, but they add to the appeal of the overall look. Since begonias span such a range of sizes, depending upon the type you choose, be sure to inquire about the mature height when purchasing your plants. All begonias prefer dry rather than moist roots.

■ BRACHYCOME / Swan River Daisy

Height 8 inches, cascading
Sun

Native to Australia, the Swan River daisy isn't fussy about the weather. You'll need bright sun to keep the sprawling, lacy leaves smothered in purple-petaled, yellow-centered, daisylike blossoms throughout the summer. Otherwise, this plant makes few demands. Don't overwater your window box when *Brachycome* is a resident. And don't worry about wedging a Swan River daisy into a crowded box; it will thrive no matter how tightly you squeeze it between neighbors.

■ BROWALLIA

Height 1 foot
Sun

Why don't more people select this blue bloomer for their red, white, and blue window boxes? Not only are the flowers dark blue, they're star-shaped as well. What could be more patriotic? Although browallia will wilt when water is not forthcoming, it snaps back when you quench its thirst, as long as the negligence hasn't been too prolonged.

Browallias should be pinched to encourage branching, and they demand bright light to keep the blossoms coming. In addition to the standard blue, there is a white form. All browallias can be grown easily from seed.

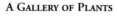

- ## BULBS

Height 6 inches to 2 feet, depending upon variety
Partial sun or shade

Who says that window boxes must be solely a summer affair? Late winter to early spring is when you need blossoms the most. Few gardening tasks are as fulfilling as planting spring bulbs in ordinary garden soil in a window box in the fall, storing them through the winter in an unheated garage or shed, then bringing them up to sit on your sill the moment growth begins. Even though snow may still persist, you can enjoy a harbinger of spring.

The beauty of bulbs is that they are no trouble whatsoever. You plant them several inches deep in the soil, store the window box in a dark garage, watering it whenever the soil goes dry, and wait for the shoots to magically appear, as they almost always do. And before too long, the flower spikes will be swelling.

Narcissus are the most gratifying window-box bulbs. They are reliable, dramatic, and long-lasting. The dwarf varieties are usually recommended for this purpose, but all the early bloomers will work. Many other spring bulbs are appropriate, especially hyacinths, snowdrops, and grape hyacinths. Tulips and crocus can also be forced, but they are fleeting.

- ## CALADIUMS

Height 1 to 1½ feet
Shade

In dense shade, caladiums provide ornately patterned foliage. In fact, the heart-shaped leaves are so large and colorful that it's difficult to put caladiums with other plants in a window box, for they generally steal the show. It may be more effective to grow caladiums of different colors with one another. Or simply display several plants of one variety lined up in regal splendor.

Caladiums come from tubers, which sprout in no time and quickly fill in to become an impressive show. Keep in mind that every leaf will be 8 inches to a foot in width, so space the plants accordingly.

Caladiums will burn in bright sun, but their ornamental leaves are wonderful where direct sunbeams don't hit.

▪ CELOSIA

Height 1 to 2 feet
Sun

Celosias are definitely daring. Not only are the colors uncompromisingly vivid, the flower shapes are quite bizarre. If you don't mind stepping out on a limb, if racy red and steamy yellow are the colors you need to add a little zing to your window box, then tuck in a few celosias.

The foliage of celosias provides scant hint of the drama that occurs the moment the plant bursts open with cockscomb- or plume-shaped flower spikes, depending upon the hybrid you choose. Transplant celosias into your box with great care, for their roots dislike being disrupted. Don't neglect a watering — they are not forgiving of drought. And they need unrelenting sun to thrive. Most folks use them sparingly as an accent — too many celosias could bring on eye-strain!

Chrysanthemums are among autumn's many pleasures. Give them as much sun as possible and don't neglect watering.

▪ CHRYSANTHEMUMS

Height 1 to 2 feet

Sun or partial sun

When autumn arrives, chrysanthemums are omnipresent in window boxes throughout the land. At a time when few other plants are in bloom, chrysanthemums burst forth. Their colors aren't particularly exuberant, but in autumn a muted window box may be quite pleasing, in contrast to the brilliant fall foliage that keeps your eyes busy.

Chrysanthemums are wonderfully easy to care for. Most people just let them bloom on, forgetting them until a killing frost renders the plant a total eyesore. A better plan is to remove the spent flowers as they fade, thus encouraging more bud formation. If the weather doesn't turn sharply cold, you can extend the blooming season for a considerable time by deadheading. Other than that one chore, you're home free. Chrysanthemums don't wilt easily, and they usually look picture-perfect with no intervention.

- ■ **COLEUS**

Height 1 to 2½ feet
Sun or shade

If you want to create a riot of color, coleus is the plant for you. The leaves can be neon yellow or deep maroon, splotched with blood red, or dappled like confetti. You can go wild mixing colors and creating vivid combinations. One thing is guaranteed; when you work with the new coleus varieties, no one in the neighborhood will have a window box quite like yours.

A word of caution: some coleus hybrids stretch to truly impressive proportions, and that isn't a positive trait for a window box plant. So steer clear of the giants; choose the dwarf varieties instead. Even then, pruning is essential to keep any coleus within bounds.

Coleus are now bred to tolerate both sun and shade. However, they tend to wilt dramatically, and they don't bounce back. So reserve these colorful plants for boxes that can be frequently watered.

- ■ **COREOPSIS**

Height 18 inches
Sun

The beauty of coreopsis is that they're dependable. No matter what the weather is during the growing season, they will blossom, which is why they've become a mainstay of perennial borders. Pale butter yellow *Coreopsis verticillata* 'Moonbeam' and its diminutive, brighter canary yellow cousin 'Zagreb' are perfect window-box fare. Unlike most perennials, they bloom nonstop throughout the summer if you deadhead them as necessary. Give them plenty of room to spread, water them regularly (although they rarely wilt), and provide as much sun as possible. Though dependable, coreopsis aren't soloists. Instead, use them as fillers to accent your more dramatic plants.

- **DIASCIA** / Twinspur
  Height 6 to 14 inches
  Sun

Although the quaint blossoms of twinspur are not large, something about them definitely tugs at your heartstrings. A profusion of these spurred blooms tumbling down makes quite a display. The diascia of greatest renown, 'Ruby Field', has vivid pink blossoms that cascade loosely on a confusion of flimsy stems over an extended time. But there are other varieties waiting in the wings for their fling with fame. Expect *Diascia rigescens,* topped by foxtail-like spires dense with coral pink blooms, to step into the limelight soon. Also keep an eye out for 'Apricot', a salmon-colored variation on the theme.

Don't be misled by their delicate-looking stems and tender-looking leaves; diascias are wonderfully long-lasting. They need sun and don't like to be over-watered, but they make few other demands. Diascias tend to rot if overcrowded, so give them plenty of space.

- **EVOLVULUS**
  Height 6 inches
  Sun

Not all members of the morning glory family will work in a window box. The 'Heavenly Blue' types, for example, wilt too easily. But *Evolvulus glomeratus* is well qualified for the position. Like its climbing counterpart, evolvulus has sky blue blossoms. But unlike its climbing kin, this little bloomer sprawls downward on a mop of furry stems. Not only do the nickel-sized blossoms keep coming throughout the summer, they remain open all day rather than unfurling only in the morning.

You would have to be terribly negligent with your watering chores to cause evolvulus to wilt even slightly. This plant stubbornly refuses to suffer. On the other hand, it doesn't like constant drenching. In a very wet summer you might experience stem rot. So plant evolvulus where it will be sheltered from roof runoff. Evolvulus is definitely a sun worshipper; you'll never see flowers if you place the box in shade.

Persian violet, fragrant and colorful, forms a neat, compact mound that flowers without pause throughout the summer.

▪ EXACUM / Persian Violet

Height 1 foot
Sun

This little performer, easily grown from seed, produces such a profusion of blossoms that you'll scarcely see the shiny, thumbnail-sized leaves. The performance begins when the plants are quite young and doesn't end until the season draws to a close. And consider the color — royal purple petals with a yellow beak in the center that just begs to be matched with something akin to 'Canary Bird' nasturtiums or the velvety foliage of *Helichrysum* 'Limelight'.

This is a tidy plant that prefers not to be scrunched in with other plants; when jammed, the stems may rot. So give it plenty of space. Also, if it's overwatered, the stems may succumb. So water your exacum lightly and give it plenty of sun to encourage a superabundance of blooms.

■ **FELICIA** / Blue Marguerite

Height 2 feet
Sun

True blue is hard to find. So felicia, with its periwinkle blue petals surrounding a yellow center, is a rare treasure for your window box. Felicia isn't easy to transplant, but once established comfortably in its container, the plant will withstand all sorts of weather. If felicia had its druthers, it would choose full sun. In a sunny spot you'll enjoy a continual supply of those precious blue flowers.

Since few blossoms can match the color of felicia, you shouldn't attempt to mix it with other blues. Instead try pink diascias or match the yellow eye with gazania 'Sundrop'. The plant likes to spread, so don't hamper its progress. Instead, choose low-growing bedfellows that will crouch around its knees. If you are fond of variegation, try the variegated *Felicia amelloides,* which has cream and green leaves.

■ **FUCHSIA**

Height 2 to 3 feet, depending upon hybrid
Shade

Fuchsias are wonderful, but they need the shade of a porch overhang. Without the shade, they'll forever look wilted. All sorts of fuchsias are available. For window boxes, however, the miniature types work best. You might consider 'Bluette', 'Buttons and Bows', 'Little Jewel', 'Papoose', or 'Tom Thumb'. Another window-box favorite is 'Honeysuckle', because of its long red flowers, burgundy leaves, and blooming persistence.

Where light levels are low, fuchsias fill the summer with blossoms. 'Cascade' assumes a trailing posture with little encouragement.

▪ HEDERA HELIX / English Ivy
Cascading
Shade

Instead of thinking of ivies as a last resort, explore the many different types available. Not only are there plain green ivies in all shapes under the sun, but there are silver- and gold-flecked, spotted, and marbled varieties. What could be more suited to showering down from an upper-story window box? Ivies are custom-made for the city, where light is scarce.

Let your ivies take the front seat in a window box so they can swoop down over the sides, with impatiens or primroses in the rear. In no time the foliage will completely camouflage the container. If your window box resides in very dense shade, where no bloomer could possibly succeed, plant a box solely with ivies in different shades and shapes. You won't be disappointed.

▪ HELICHRYSUM
Height 1 foot
Sun

At last helichrysums are receiving the fame that is their due. Bred for hot, sunny environments, helichrysums hold their own when everything else wilts. If you put them in a terra cotta window box baking in brilliant sun, they won't bat an eye. If you neglect to water them for a day or so, they'll bounce back. Helichrysums are fabulous for window boxes. It's little wonder that so many have recently been introduced.

The best choice for a window box is *Helichrysum petiolare,* also known as licorice plant for no apparent reason (the foliage does not taste, smell, or look like licorice). The rounded leaves are plush, velvety silver (children love to pat the foliage), and the plants cascade gracefully from the rim of a window box. Rarely used alone, *Helichrysum petiolare* generally accompanies an upright bloomer such as felicia. Equally useful is the lime green hybrid 'Limelight'. In fact, the two look very handsome together. Steer away from the variegated version, for it is prone to stem rot. And explore other types as well, such as *Helichrysum* 'Moe's Gold', and *Helichrysum bracteatum* — strawflower — grown for its globelike dry flowers.

Helichrysums like the soil to dry out between waterings, but they prefer not to be parched. They should be pruned quite stringently to promote branching.

■ HELIOTROPIUM / Heliotrope
Height 1 foot
Sun

If it's fragrance that you crave, heliotrope is the plant for you. In full sun, it flowers continually, emitting a perfume reminiscent of baby powder steeped in vanilla. If you grow 'Iowa', that elixir will be combined with the essence of mulled cider as well. These heady plants are well worth a place outside anyone's window.

Fragrance is not their only attribute; the flowers are handsome as well. Choose the deep purple or the snow white version, or mix the two together. One word of caution: 'Princess Marina' has very little scent.

Heliotropes demand sun and they need to be watered religiously. They wilt easily and drop their leaves as a result. The watering can should never be far away, and you should be at the ready with the shears. If they aren't pruned, heliotropes look shabby. But they blossom quickly after being cut back.

■ HERBS
Varying heights
Sun

Numerous herbs are suitable to window boxes; space doesn't permit a complete inventory with a description of each one. I'll concentrate on the herbs that work best in window boxes. Most gardeners like to grow culinary herbs close to the kitchen so they can harvest them rapidly when the menu calls for some herbal seasoning. In addition to those old standards parsley, sage, rosemary, and thyme, a culinary window box might hold a combination of chives, summer or winter savory, marjoram, oregano, and fine-leaved basil. Not only will your window box residents taste delicious, they will emit enticing scents when you brush the leaves.

Of course, cooking is just one area in which herbs make themselves useful. You could compose a medicinal window box with aloe, comfrey, lavender, and rosemary. Or you can just enjoy the beauty of herbs such as the ornamental salvias, flowering oreganos, lamb's-ears, and dianthus.

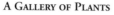

Most herbs prefer sun, and as a rule, they like to dry out between water-ings — which makes them perfect recruits for the window box. If you plant several herbs together, try to mix trailers, such as savory and thyme, with upright plants, such as rosemary. Most important, give them all plenty of space.

■ IMPATIENS

Height 1 to 2 feet
Shade

Few plants are as impressive in a window box as impatiens. They blossom with an energy that leaves other bloomers panting in their dust, and they require very little work. Most types are self-branching, although a little work with the shears will encourage them in the proper direction. Even after severe pruning, an impatiens bounces back to produce quantities of blossoms, each an inch or so in diameter. If you select *Impatiens wallerana,* you can easily grow the plants from seed and have a rhapsody in shades of pink. Recently a miniature strain known as the Hawaiian series has been introduced, with blossoms so plentiful that they completely carpet the foliage. Other new compact impatiens produce an abundance of rosebud-shaped flowers.

Impatiens does not tolerate a lot of sun; they will wilt with devastating rapidity no matter how much water you pour on. Even in shade they require a generous supply of water. However, the New Guinea hybrids, which come in a rainbow of colors including white, pink, salmon, red, lavender, purple, and orange, are happy in a sunny spot.

■ IPOMOEA

Vining
Sun

Contrast can be the key to a great window box. If you play silver against deep burgundy, the result is particularly compliment-fetching. If that's your plan, *Ipomoea batatas* 'Blackie' is perfect. Although this relative of the sweet potato doesn't blossom, it boasts deeply cleft leaves of the darkest purple you can imagine, verging on black. The shape is rather interesting, but it is the color that makes this vine valuable. In a dark window box, the dramatic trailing leaves would be

Double impatiens look like a bountiful crop of rosebuds. 'Double Amethyst' is particularly prolific.

lost. But in a concrete container or white wooden box, they stand out admirably.

Ipomoea batatas 'Blackie' will grow in partial sun, but it performs best with good light. It rarely wilts, but the leaves may drop in a severe drought, so don't tempt fate. 'Blackie' tends to send down one long, lean shoot. To encourage more shoots to sprout from the base, pinch the plant when you put it in the window box. And use it sparingly — one or two plants will make a strong statement.

Content in a variety of locations, Lamium maculatum *'White Nancy' produces both blossoms and luminous leaves in sun or shade.*

■ **LAMIUM**

Height 1 foot
Partial sun or shade

Lamiums have several good features. The luminous pearly white foliage of 'Pink Pewter', 'Beacon Silver', and 'White Nancy' is pleasing to the eye. And throughout the summer, the plants are studded with closely held heads of blossoms. 'Pink Pewter' and 'Beacon Silver' have pink blooms; those of 'White Nancy' are swan-colored.

In the ground this perennial has a reputation for being invasive. But in a window box it doesn't have sufficient time to become a bully. It just fills in rather rapidly. Still, it's best not to plant it beside something that can't hold its ground. Not only will lamiums tolerate quite dense shade and bloom prolifically, they can withstand some rather lengthy droughts without wilting. Such behavior should definitely be applauded.

■ **LANTANA**

Height 1 to 2 feet
Sun

Those of us who want instant gratification turn to lantanas, which start their blooming cycle when they are merely a few inches tall. And the performance really never ends throughout the growing season. The flowers come in all shades, from blushing coral and yellow together, in *Lantana camara,* to purple, in the trailing *Lantana montevidensis,* to pearly white, in *Lantana montevidensis* 'Alba'. They bloom long and blossom heavily; with generous sun, lantanas are always densely laden.

The plants can go thirsty for a while without swooning. The stiff, impermeable leaves emit a rather musky scent that has earned the plant the nickname polecat geranium. But the flowers make up for this infraction with their candy-like perfume. Lantanas are energetic; pruning is compulsory at the beginning of this plant's window-box career, as is a major snipping back halfway through the season.

■ **PELARGONIUM**

Height 1 to 2 feet
Sun

Don't be put off by the long Latin name. The plants I'm talking about here are those we all know and love as geraniums. Whatever the name, these colorful bloomers are legendary for their performance in window boxes. Granted, the cherry red zonal geranium has become a little overdone lately. But there are plenty of other colors available — try playing with white, pink, magenta, salmon, or orange, mixed with something more daring than alyssum and lobelia. You might experiment with other types of pelargoniums, such as ivy geraniums or the various scented-leaved geraniums. They are equally amiable.

Pelargoniums need sun and plenty of it. They also need pruning and water on a regular basis. They tend to spread out, so be generous with your spacing — especially with the ivy geraniums. Other than that, these plants are quite accommodating.

■ **PETUNIA**

Height 1 foot
Sun

Who can fail to fall for a petunia? They're incredibly happy-go-lucky bloomers. You plant them in a window box, and they just go about the business of producing lots of big, showy flowers. And consider the colors available — every shade of the rainbow is represented in this genus. There are even bicolor petunias with beach-ball stripes. If you're a connoisseur, plant the magenta everbloomer, *Petunia integrifolia.*

The secret to growing great petunia window boxes seems to be nestling plenty of plants close together. That way they push each other upward — you get height as well as length dangling down. Another trick is to prune the plants early on and deadhead spent blossoms quickly. Petunias wilt easily, so don't neglect to water. Most important, give them full sun.

■ **PRIMULA** / Primrose

Height 6 to 12 inches
Shade

The only problem with primroses in a window box is that they don't last long enough. For a few glorious weeks in spring you can enjoy a truly delightful display, then the show is over. Several varieties of primroses are suitable for window boxes; among the most popular are the widely available hybrids as well as *Primula denticulata,* with tall drumstick-like flower heads in varying shades of pink, blue, purple, and white. *Primula veris* has clusters of flowers on each stem, in all colors of the rainbow, surrounded by a rosette of leaves. They look like little nosegays, and their fragrance fulfills the analogy.

Primroses do have their problems. Fetching water to keep the foliage from wilting can be a full-time job. And if your box is in full sun, woe to the primulas in residence. Then there's the issue of red spider mites; those pests are drawn to primroses from all corners of the earth. Fortunately, mites detest cool damp conditions. So if you keep your primroses well watered, the problem should heal itself. Primroses are fine for spring, but plan to replant your window box when the days begin to warm up.

In partial shade, primroses of all types thrive and blossom until the weather becomes warm.

■ **SALVIA**

Height 1¹/₂ to 3 feet
Sun

Salvias are certainly one of the most diverse groups of plants you can think of for a window box. They come in all heights, shapes, and sizes, and a variety of leaf textures and colors. The color range of the blossoms is incredibly wide; there's not a shade that isn't represented. An affection for sun seems to be shared by all plants in this genus.

The most common salvia for window boxes is *Salvia splendens,* with its spires of fire-engine-red flowers. Because it is tall (to 3 feet), it should stay at the rear of the box.

The leaves and flower structure of *Salvia vanhouttii* are similar, but rather than screaming red, the blossoms are a much more palatable shade of deep burgundy, emerging from darker calyxes. The foliage of both *S. superba* and *S. vanhouttii* wilts with little provocation, so water must be regularly applied.

If you aren't ever-ready with the watering pot, there are other salvias for you. *Salvia chamaedryoides* is a cascading little bloomer with sailor blue blossoms and satiny silver leaves on wiry stems. The beauty of this species is its drought tolerance. *Salvia greggii* and *Salvia × jamensis* are also willing to withstand some thirst, and their colors range from moonlight yellow through salmon, peach, and pink to maraschino red. However, these types tend to grow into a blowzy cloud of bloom unless you control them with some strategic cuts. Another solution is to tuck the plants close together to counteract the loose effect.

■ **SCABIOSA** / Pincushion Flower

Height 1¹/₂ to 2 feet
Sun

Most pincushion-flower varieties are too tall for the average window box. But the dwarf 'Butterfly Blue' is well within bounds. And it blossoms throughout the spring and summer, which is a virtue that few perennials share. The plant crouches low, but the flower wands rise a foot above, holding their flat cushions of blooms proudly for the world to see. These cushions are quite pretty in both form and

Although Salvia splendens *(combined with impatiens here) is the variety most often used in containers, many other salvias work equally effectively.*

color — each flower head is 2 inches in diameter, with baby blue petals. A combination of blue scabiosa and something with pale pink flowers is heavenly.

Scabiosa requires sun, and it doesn't wilt quickly. Best of all, it's a tidy plant with scarcely a leaf out of place or off-color. Don't hesitate to profile it prominently. Or use it as a well-behaved accent to fill some empty crevices.

The felted leaves of Stachys byzantina, *lamb's-ears, attract children to fondle the foliage and appreciate your bite-sized garden.*

- ### SCAEVOLA / Fan Flower
  Height 1 foot
  Cascading
  Sun

For good reason, the fan flower has taken the gardening world by storm. There's scarcely a job that this eager purple bloomer hasn't been asked to accomplish. And it gladly does any task, as long as the position is sunny. It seems most content in a container, perhaps because it prefers to dry out between waterings. A large window box is best, for a single plant of scaevola will spread out to take up a generous foot in all directions. Even then it might be cramped unless you position it front and center to cascade gracefully over the rim. Each blossom is only an inch in size, but the plant flowers so profusely that it is smothered in purple throughout the summer. Steer away from the white form that has recently been introduced, for it is not as enduring as the purple variety; the flowers shatter a day or so after they open. Some good things can't be improved.

Scaevola blooms best when the sun is intense, but it will wilt when watering has been neglected — and you can't call its bluff too many times. The plant is self-branching, but you might want to encourage that tendency with a little shearing.

- ### STACHYS / Lamb's-Ears
  Height 1½ feet
  Sun or shade

If you have a child or a grandchild, or if you are just young at heart, put lamb's-ears in a window box within easy reach. It's one of those plants that just has to be touched. Patting the plush foliage can be therapeutic. No question about it, the leaves are the main attraction with *Stachys byzantina* — and they're definitely the primary reason why this simple plant has been adapted as an ornamental. The porcelain pink blossoms that peek out from those furry spikes combine well with other flowers — *Diascia* 'Ruby Field' comes to mind immediately. In fact, you should combine lamb's-ears with something that will cascade in front of it; when the plant puts its energy into flower spikes, it can

become a little naked around the ankles. Or carry the plush silver foliage theme one step further by camouflaging those ankles with *Plecostachys serpyllifolia,* the miniature licorice plant.

Give lamb's-ears sun or shade, drench it heavily or forget to water once in a while, and it will grow on nevertheless. These plants are nearly indestructible.

■ TAGETES / Marigold
Height 1 to 3 feet, depending upon variety
Sun

There's no need to devote an entire box to marigolds, although that is often done. Instead, if you like bright neon yellow, tuck a marigold or two in with coreopsis or the chocolate cosmos. Marigolds are famed for their window-box feats. In no time they have filled in completely and are happily blooming their little hearts out. You can water them liberally or neglectfully, you can give them the worst growing conditions possible, and they will stubbornly persist in blossoming. My first Brownie project as a child was to grow a marigold window box. The fact that it thrived is a good indication of the plant's fortitude.

Although marigolds have a forgiving nature, you should put the French dwarf varieties, which are especially well suited for window boxes, in full sun to keep them from stretching. People tend to squeeze them into any little pocket in the box that requires brightening up. This leads to weak stems and toppling over. Generous spacing will solve the problem.

■ VERBENA
Height 1 foot
Sun

Verbenas are frequently used in window boxes. Their blossom rosettes are large, and they come in a range of colors from pink, salmon, white, and red to blue and purple. There are also bicolors available, such as the blue-and-white-striped 'Carousel'. You see them cascading gracefully, their stems flowing down with those glorious blossoms dangling at the tips. This is a sight that instills envy. And

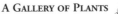

if you choose a hybrid such as 'Silver Anne' or 'Carousel', you'll find it fragrant as well.

A verbena extravaganza is not a vision that you can create without effort. First of all, you must prune them early to encourage branching. And you've got to be persistent with the shears. Since verbenas bloom at the tips, when you pinch them back, you'll forfeit blossoms so you have to deny yourself some early pleasures. But eventually the plant will assume the proper posture and flowers will be forthcoming.

You can't neglect the necessary constant watering, for verbenas wilt in a blink. And they demand full sun, or the plants will be leggy and blossoms nil. One further word of caution: verbenas sunburn easily when you first plant them outside. So put them out for a short time in partial shade, then gradually increase the amount of sun they get. And watch out for red spider mites. By following these few rules you'll have a dazzling display.

■ VIOLAS AND PANSIES
Height 6 inches
Shade

Spring can't be said to have arrived until window boxes spilling with violas and pansies appear on everyone's front porch. And who can resist playing around with combinations of those pert-faced flowers, each accented by quaint black whiskers? Many sorts of pansies are available — you'll have a wonderful time mixing colors and combining the tiny Johnny-jump-ups with larger-flowering hybrids. There is scarcely a shade that isn't well represented in the viola repertoire.

Viola and pansy window boxes are perfect for the beginner, though light can be a little baffling. They blossom best in partial shade but will become straggly without enough light. By trying different locations, you'll soon arrive at the right balance. A well-situated viola window box is worth the time spent experimenting. Unfortunately, violas don't last forever. When the weather gets hot, the plants begin to grow leggy and should be replaced. Granted, the flowers will persist. But you want your window box to look absolutely magnificent. So when your pansies begin to stretch, replant with another intriguing combination of plants.

HARDINESS ZONE MAP

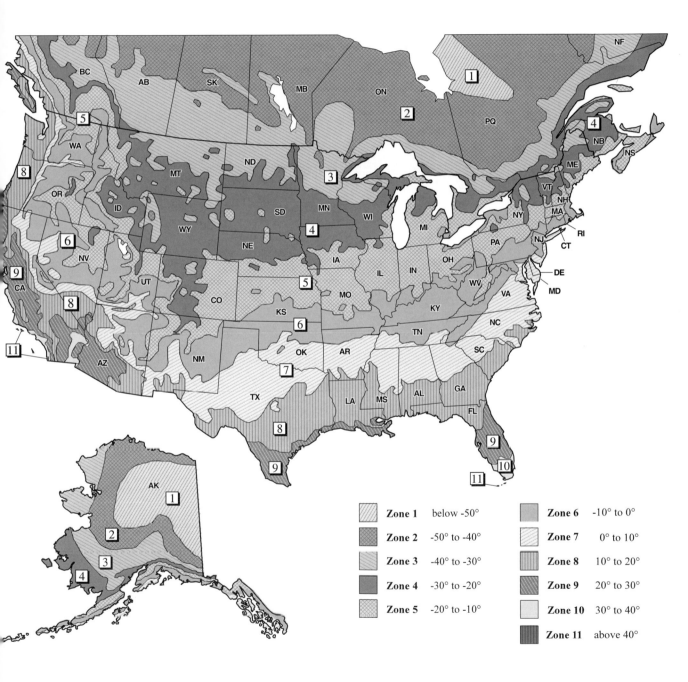

	Zone 1	below -50°		Zone 6	-10° to 0°
	Zone 2	-50° to -40°		Zone 7	0° to 10°
	Zone 3	-40° to -30°		Zone 8	10° to 20°
	Zone 4	-30° to -20°		Zone 9	20° to 30°
	Zone 5	-20° to -10°		Zone 10	30° to 40°
				Zone 11	above 40°

Photo Credits

Cathy Wilkinson Barash: iii, 36

Karen Bussolini: 52–53, 56–57

Priscilla Connell/Photo/Nats: 6, 40–41

Thomas Eltzroth: 15, 30–31

Derek Fell: vi–1, 82, 88–89, 109

Charles Marden Fitch: 44–45, 64

Lynne Harrison: 38, 74–75

Margaret Hensel/Positive Images: 7

Jerry Howard/Positive Images: 8

Andrew Lawson: 10–11, 25, 28–29, 33, 34, 47, 50, 60–61, 66–67

Charles Mann: 24

Rick Mark: 3, 4–5, 93

Tovah Martin: 85, 90, 98, 99, 103

Rick Mastelli: 2, 76–77, 87, 104, 107, 110, back cover

John Neubauer: 20–21

PhotoSynthesis: 23, 26, 48

George Taloumis: 12–13, 16, 17, 18, 43, 55, 69, 70–71, 72, 80, 94–95

Michael S. Thompson: 58

INDEX

Page numbers in italics refer to illustrations.

Titles available in the Taylor's Weekend Gardening Guides series:

Organic Pest and Disease Control	$12.95
Safe and Easy Lawn Care	12.95
Window Boxes	12.95
Attracting Birds and Butterflies	12.95
Water Gardens	12.95
Pruning	12.95

At your bookstore or by calling 1-800-225-3362

Prices subject to change without notice